D1435349

SUN TZU'S ANCIENT ART OF GOLF™

Translated (with commentary)
by Gary Parker Chapin
and T. Liam McDonald

ILLUSTRATED BY BRUCE JORGENSEN

CB

CONTEMPORARY
BOOKS

CHICAGO

Library of Congress Cataloging-in-Publication Data

Chapin, Gary Parker.
    Sun tzu's ancient art of golf / translated with
commentary by Gary Parker Chapin and T. Liam
McDonald.
       p.   cm.
    ISBN 0-8092-3838-1
    1. Golf—Humor.   2. Sun-tzu, 6th cent. B.C.—
Parodies, imitations, etc.   I. McDonald, T.
Liam.   II. Title.
PN6231.G68C43   1992
818'.5407—dc20   92-25840
                                        CIP

Published by Contemporary Books, Inc.
180 North Michigan Avenue, Chicago, Illinois 60601
Manufactured in the United States of America
International Standard Book Number: 0-8092-3838-1

To Mike The Golf Pro
Sun

To Ellis Parker Butler, for the first inspiration,
and to Sheryl, for all kinds of great reasons
Chapin

To my parents, for making it all possible,
and to Elizabeth, for making it all worth having
McDonald

And, of course,
to
P. G. Wodehouse,
for showing us how it's done

Foreword

Sun Tzu is undoubtedly known to many of you as the ancient Chinese scribe[1] of the Ancient Kingdom of Wu[2] who put together that topping little pamphlet, *The Ancient Art of War*.[3] This booklet excited just the type of person who takes joy in knocking opposing armored tank divisions into next week; or that sort of gentleman who makes it a point not to eat breakfast before bayoneting at least thirty other gentlemen who happen to be on the "other side."

---

[1]Roughly equivalent to a present-day Chinese scribe, only older.

[2]Roughly equivalent to the present-day Kingdom of Wu, only older.

[3]Actually, we aren't quite sure if Sun Tzu wrote a pamphlet called *The Ancient Art of War* or if he merely wrote a pamphlet, which is currently *ancient*, called *The Art of War*. Our copy is copyrighted 1985 by the honorable Sterling House Publishers, and, frankly, that doesn't strike either of us as being that old, let alone ancient.

Further, many found Mr. Sun's dollop of wisdom to be applicable to other modes of life. Lawyers, literary agents, publishers, students, football players, et al.—all give Mr. Sun high marks in the category of *applicability to situation, current.* In fact, we know of at least one greatly admired businessman who wouldn't think of conducting a bit of corporate raiding without first consulting Mr. Sun on, say, the use of spies as a viable and cost-effective business tactic.[4] Alas, Mr. Sun, wise though he was, appeared to have few words for those of us interested in more civilized activities.

We speak, of course, of golf: that noble pastime, that indispensable sport, that religion masquerading as a game.

For there is little in Mr. Sun's sagacious brochure that would get one out of that vast abyss that borders the fairway on the seventh at St. Boxley's Golf Heaven, the Bronx. Even less that would aid one in clearing the hellishly placed bunkers at Hoboken Greens, New Jersey. Sad as it is to say, *Sun Tzu's Ancient Art of War* fails to address even the very basics of golf. Did the old man ever discourse upon the salient points of the short game, propound on the proper methods of dealing with a nasty slice,

---

[4]Sun says, "There is no place in which espionage is not possible." And a good thing, too, since the gentleman—who spoke to us under the condition of anonymity—currently resides in the New York State Minimum Security Correctional Facility (four stars), and, yes, continues to consult his Sun Tzu on a daily basis.

or discuss the varied benefits of the interlocking grip[5]? No. In fact, there is not a single dollop of wisdom—nay, not even a single footnote or parenthetical aside—from Sun Tzu that even *mentions* the word "golf"!

Or so it was thought.

* * *

The tale of the discovery of the text in question is amazing, if brief. Your translators were on their customary and annual sabbatical, having decided to take in the much acclaimed "Great Golf Courses of the Far East" package offered by one of the more discriminating, if less sanitary, chartered airline companies. We had just finished nine of the eighteen at the Ancient Kingdom of Wu Golf-O-Rama[6] and had decided to have a drink in the clubhouse before continuing on our round.

At the bar—decorated in a tasteful (really) gold and red motif—we were in the process of consuming some appropriately bizarre mixed-drink concoctions while silently running over our respective strategies for the back nine. As we readied to lift our elbows for a final slug before we slogged onward, Mr. Chapin noticed that the swizzle stick had

---

[5]"Used by all your best players," says Mike The Golf Pro.

[6]You've probably heard of it. It's the course with that whacking huge Great Wall cutting right through the middle of the long sixteenth. Damnable nuisance of a hazard, we think.

dropped out of his drink and fallen behind the bar. There being no bartender-type individual to gather it up for him, it was but the work of a moment for Chapin to walk behind and bend down to pick the thing up himself.

Mr. McDonald was not a little shocked when he then heard Chapin gasp and wheeze like one of those plastic squeeze bottles of catsup that has been drained to the almost-last drop.

"Hold on a minute!" said Chapin, before doing more of that wheezing thing.

McDonald held on—expecting to do so for the full sixty—but less than a minute had gone by when Chapin shot up from behind the bar, threw a handful of swizzle sticks at McDonald, and asked, "What do you make of this?!"

McDonald looked at the swizzle sticks—nice little bamboo structures, each a few inches long and a quarter-inch wide—and said, "Oh, I don't know, probably a nice house, or a toy boat, or a straw man—but really, Gary, now is not the time." The two were on cordial terms, even though McDonald was a triple-bogey nuisance.

"No, no, no," Chapin expelled, a little wild-eyed and foaming. "No. I mean the *writing* on the sticks!"

"Oh!" McDonald hadn't noticed any of said writing, but yes, indeed, each little bamboo swizzle stick had a few Chinese characters written in a faded, bluish ink. McDonald looked at the sticks, feeling very fortunate that he had taken that adult education course in Chinese (Ancient Kingdom of Wu dialect). Still, the writing was faded, the penmanship atrocious, and the whole thing was tough going.

But after a few minutes he'd made out the characters on one of the slivers, and read it, haltingly, "Keep . . . your . . . hen? . . . heck? . . . No! Head! Keep your head still!" he announced triumphantly.

Keep your head still.

We looked at each other, stunned. The most important bit of advice that any golfer can clasp to his bosom, that first and most crucial Commandment, found written in an ancient hand on a swizzle stick in the Kingdom of Wu, China?

What went on here?

It was quick work to look through the rest of the sticks, McDonald translating, Chapin scratching notes. Some of the slivers were mere fragments, making no sense at all (*Fozzling hacks . . .*); some were full declarations that in Western form are held as The Truth among golfers to this very day (*He who plants his feet like the hibiscus will avoid the dreaded reverse pivot*); indeed, some were hints on playing the very course that we were battling through at the moment (*He who stands too close to the ball on the seventh will hook, and hook badly.* And we had both hooked, badly!).

Finally, McDonald pulled out the shard that told all.

"Wait a minute," he said.

ANCIENT GOLF RULE NUMBER ONE:
KEEP YOUR HEAD STILL.

Chapin waited.

A full minute later McDonald continued, "Copywrite . . . no, no . . . copyright! That's it! Copyright five . . . hundred . . . B.C. . . . hold on, I can't make out the name. Copyright 500 B.C. . . . Sun Tzu." McDonald was sweating with the effort.

Copyright 500 B.C. Sun Tzu.

"Five hundred B.C., eh?" said Chapin. "That would put the thing in public domain, wouldn't it?"

We looked at each other with that look that says, "Oh, my. We've stumbled over something quite large and profitable, haven't we?" And we began gathering up every swizzle stick in the clubhouse. One hour later we were on a plane heading back to New Jersey—where Chapin held an associate professorship in Convincing the Federal Government to Give Us Vastly Huge Sums of Money at Hoboken Community College—with nearly one thousand bamboo swizzle sticks concealed in the linings of our carry-on luggage and taped all over our bodies[7]. Once back in the U.S. we got a vastly huge grant from the federal government and set about translating and organizing what we like to call *The Old Chinese Guy Takes You Through Your Strokes*.[8]

---

[7]That was the only way we could slip the things through customs. Apparently bamboo swizzle sticks are a heavily controlled export item for the Chinese.

[8]But the publishers want to call it *Sun Tzu's Ancient Art of Golf*, so that's what's on the cover. To be honest, though, we really don't think it's got that *zing*.

* * *

It's not often that one is able to introduce to the modern world an ancient text of indisputable power and relevance. The Dead Sea Scrolls, the Gnostic texts, a first edition of *The Man from U.N.C.L.E. and the Despicable Wench*—each is a sacred tome of quite massive importance, but in terms of real-world value and day-to-day significance *Sun Tzu's Ancient Art of Golf* has got it over those moldy documents hands down.

Yes, there are some historians who will scoff. "How," they will say, "can an ancient Chinese scribe write in the fourth century B.C. on golf when the game wasn't even invented until the fourteenth century A.D.? Hah!" they will chortle. "Hah! Explain that!"

To these people we say, "The same way he was able to write on hostile corporate takeovers when *that* game wasn't invented (or at least perfected) until the twentieth century A.D.—*the man had vision.*" So there. They'll have to come up with better than that to dissuade us of the veracity of the venerable Mr. Sun.

Anyway, for this book we have chosen to bypass the question of the bamboo sticks' authenticity,[9] preferring merely to present the text and let The Words speak for themselves. We do comment occa-

---

[9]There has, however, been some interesting speculation on this point. The authors feel that P. G. Wodehouse's "fictional" story "The Coming of Gowf" offers a particularly plausible theory regarding golf migration.

ANCIENT CHINESE SCRIBE AT WORK...

sionally upon Mr. Sun's counsel, providing clarification, historical background, and testimonial regarding Mr. Sun's effects upon our chip shots and whatall. But this is only in the purest academic tradition of annotating a text to the point where it says exactly what we want it to say.

So read the words of Mr. Sun, absorb his wisdom and utilize its ancient puissance. After you've done so, we feel that this work will have more than earned its place on your bookshelf alongside those other great golfing volumes—*Clausewitz: On Golf*, Toynbee's *A Study of Golf*, and Barbara W. Tuchman's *A Distant Hole*. And all questions regarding their bona fides will be irrelevant.

We're so sure of this that we promise: If reading this book doesn't shave, say, one or two points off your game, then you'll have every right to be quite annoyed with us.[10]

The honor is yours . . .

Gary Parker Chapin
T. Liam McDonald

---

[10]But no refund.

Introduction

Why We Play Golf

"The Fairway can be known but not The True Fairway"

—Lao Tzu, after losing the Year of
the Asparagus World Cup finals

In golf, the player begins at the tee with only a club, a caddie, and a spherical reminder of his being.[11] This, truly, is the eternal trinity. It is a paradigm for existence. You begin with nothing; then you battle your way through the slings and hazards of outrageous fortune, the roughs, the bunkers, the water holes, until you finally reach the Nirvana of the green, that Holy Grail, that cup into which your ball will pleasantly fall. Thus the golfer comes to terms with his mortality every time he holes out, taking that many strokes off of the burden of his life.

---

[11]We think he means the ball.

The True Golfer cannot just keep his head down, swing the club, and hope to reach the cup. He must purify himself. He must plan and meditate upon his course of action. He must prepare himself for the battle. This can only be done by creating within himself a spiritual oneness with all things Golf: the ball, the clubs, the caddie, the green, the hole, the flag, the Pro, and even the humble bug that crawls upon his shoe.

This is most important in regards to the ball. The True Golfer must project himself into the ball, placing his mind in among the panda fur.[12] He must *see* the ball,[13] see it with his eyes closed.[14] He must be one with the ball, for the ball and the cup are already one, they need only be brought into alignment. In other words, the path between the tee and the cup already exists. It is the duty of the True Golfer to find it.

---

[12]In China they constructed their balls much the way the early Scots did, with the exception that, rather than filling a small leather pouch with enough feathers to create what they called "a ball," the ancient Chinese filled a small leather pouch with all of the hair from an adult panda, thus creating what they called "a ball." This had the side effect of producing one of the odder hazards of the ancient Chinese golf course: annoyed bald pandas. (See chapter on hazards.)

[13]Good advice!

[14]This is purely metaphorical, or else all that keep-your-head-down and keep-your-eye-on-the-ball blather would be so many yak patties.

The ball has three emotional states of being: the ball at rest, the ball in flight, and the ball irrevocably lost among the bottomless water hazards and volcanic craters. Treat it sympathetically and the dimples will align to conform with your destiny.

Remember also that the club is not a thing that is held but is actually an extension of your physical body. It is the limb that we lost when we were cast from our former Edenic existence, and for which we shall search throughout this life. Should one see the human aura, he would see it around two areas where there is no Body. These are normally where the tail and the golf club would be. This is why golf is the true sport of ancients and the One True Way. The only reason the club is no longer part of the True Golfer's anatomy is because that would preclude whispered conferences with the caddie over whether a mashie or a square-root-of-2 iron would be more appropriate.

In conclusion, let me tell this story which, I feel, will amply illustrate what is at stake in the Game of Golf: Lao Tzu, the Old Scholar who taught of *The Tao*, or *The Way*; and Confucius, the Young Scholar who wrote thousands of one-liners for fortune cookies, were on the back nine of The Royal Palace Linx (temple and prayer mat at every tee) when Lao Tzu whacked a nasty slice off the mountain. There was a prolonged silence; then Confucius said, "The one-winged bird who flies a crooked path completes his journey in due time." To which Lao Tzu answered,

"The ball is not white because of the ball washer but because of the water hazard."[15]

[15]We haven't the slightest idea why Sun Tzu would choose to end his chapter with this anecdote (in fact, we have no idea what it *means*). Sung Pu in his masterful, five volume analysis, *The Master and the Ball: Lao Tzu, the Tao, and Your Handicap*, made a noble attempt, but all he came up with was that Confucius expected Lao Tzu to play out his ball. No doubt it will keep students of philosophy writing papers well into the next millennium.

BALL WASHER -- IMPERIAL LINKS OF WU _.

1ST TEE

HOLY TRINITY OF GOLF..

1

Waging Golf

Golf is a matter of vital importance to the individual, a matter of life or death, the road to either survival or to ruin, to acclaim or to intense, heartrending embarrassment. Therefore it is vital that it be studied thoroughly and won.

To that end, I offer unto you the five fundamental factors with which one can make the comparison between yourself and your enemy at the tee. The first of these factors is home life—meaning that thing which causes the golfer to be in harmony (or disharmony) with the ball and those around him, i.e., the golfer's spouse; the second is weather—meaning rain, sun, cold, heat, humidity, snow (blizzard or just flurries), tornadoes, hurricanes,[16] long-

---

[16]Regarding storms, the editors highly recommend that the reader consult the work of Hu Chung, sixth century scribe, meteorologist, and golfer. His book, *Driving into the Wind: Turning the Monsoon to Your Advantage on the Links*, is invaluable.

moving cold fronts from Canada, cumulonimbi with bad attitudes, and other weather-type phenomena (this does not mean volcanoes, however); the third is terrain—meaning the ground, distance of, things on, and geological phenomena therein (this, truly, is where volcanoes must be listed); fourth is the golfer—meaning the golfer; fifth is equipment—meaning that whoever owns the thousand-yi[17] set of Wu Li Snead Clubs is going to have a cakewalk; this also refers to such things as battle dress, balls, and caddies; and sixth is doctrine—meaning how well you know the rules and can thus trap your opponent in the nine-fold labyrinth of the "driving into a pack of wandering Zen Masters" provision and receive from him a stroke.

These then are the five—no, wait a minute . . . two . . . four . . . six! These then are the *six* provisions by which you will be able to determine your chances of beating an opponent. Of course, if you have already stepped up to the tee when you discover that you have the same chance of winning as the humble brown squirrel has of holding up a twenty-four-hour convenience store, then you will most likely be unable to back out of the match without suffering severe social embarrassment.

These, therefore, are the three things you might do when you are unable to call off a game that is sure to become a humiliating rout: First, accept

---

[17]The *yi* is an ancient Chinese denomination of money, roughly equivalent to $3.90477464552 (Australian).

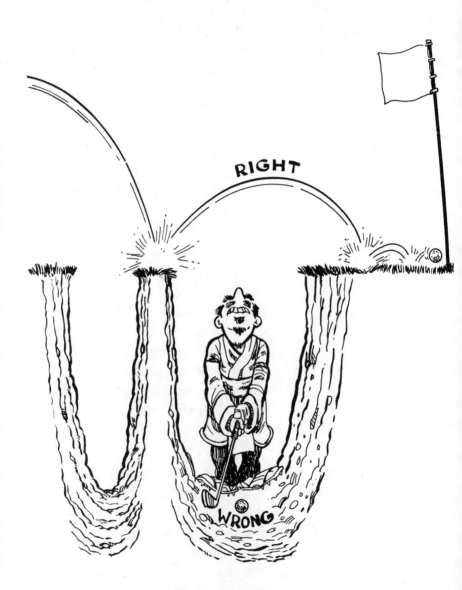

your defeat as a learning experience and remember that, as The Master says, "All golf is suffering." Second, claim that you hear your wife calling. Do this by perking up your ear and saying something like, "Is that my wife calling?" Finally, you may consult my chapter entitled "Offensive (and I Mean *Really* Offensive) Strategies" and start saving up your phlegm.

GOLF SURVEILLANCE DEVICE...

2

The Arsenal: Golf Equipment

A golfer is only as good as his equipment. He must choose it with care. It will be with him for his entire journey in this life and will accompany him to the next.

Here, then, are the five essential articles that every True Golfer will need. Treat each as though it were another limb.

The Ball: The ball must be stuffed and weighted with the Proper Material. All balls must be tested at the Beijing Center for Higher Ball Studies before they come to your local Pro Shop, so you can rest assured that they have the proper Spiritual Qualities. One should check the Local Rules at one's local golf establishment as to their requirements for ball weight, consistency, dexterity, flight capability, and political alignment. (This last changes with each dynasty.)

It is important to choose a ball that is on the

same spiritual plane as yourself. Take special note of dimple patterns, for they hold great resonance. Read them as one would read the simple tea leaves of your cup or the stars above. This will save you many strokes.

The Clubs: The rules state that a player can carry with him ninety-three clubs (the Perfect Number) of any variety or combination.[18] Carrying ninety-four will result in execution or the doubling of green fees.

---

[18]The clubs commonly in use by the ancient Chinese of Sun Tzu's time were substantially different from those clubs with which modern golfers embarrass themselves. Sun Tzu, on his trips around the thirty-one holes of the Wang Mang Reformed Memorial Pitch 'n' Putt might have used any number of the following clubs recently discovered by Professor Heinlitzt van Snorklestein in his excavation of the tomb of noted golf enthusiast (and emperor) Tang Tai Tsung (A.D. 626–649):

1. The number 43 wood, which, when tested, overshot all nine holes at St. Andrews
2. The Seven Stars and a Moon iron (no . . . we don't know either)
3. The π iron
4. A baseball bat
5. And one, whose name has not yet been deciphered, that resembles nothing so much as a cross between a pool cue, a small piece of artillery, and a tennis racket. We have a nagging suspicion that it has something to do with that Great Wall thing.

The importance of the clubs cannot be under-stressed.[19]

The Tees: I prefer a nice green tee.

The Bag: A bag is a device for holding clubs, usually made of the entire stomach of a large milk-producing bovine creature.[20] It is the environment in which your clubs will exist and is thus very important.[21] The inner life of your clubs relies heavily upon your use of the proper bag. I recommend the Wu Li Snead Bag.[22]

The Cart: Oxen are preferred, but they must wear slippers in order to prevent undue scuffing of the fairway.

The Caddie: Choosing the proper caddie is as im-portant as choosing the ball, club, tee, cart, or opponent. Your caddie will be a costly investment, particularly after such things as fees, feeding and

---

[19]We're not quite sure what Sun was getting at here, but we suggest that you take his word for it.

[20]I.e., a cow.

[21]Bags today are made of vinyl, metal, and plastic and are sure to set you back several hundred dollars and give your caddie's chiropractor reason to rejoice, not to mention ruining the karma of your clubs. It is best to make your own, so start looking for that cow.

[22]Endorsement paid for by the Committee to Elect Wu Li Snead to Lord High Imperial Greenskeeper.

⦿USING SPECIALIZED CLUBS...

watering, maintenance, tips, more feeding and watering, and paying him off for conveniently not observing those practices that are part and parcel of any True Golfer's offensive strategy.[23]

There are three criteria for choosing the proper caddie:

1. Breeding. His parents must have been members of the Caddie Class. If you cannot afford the well-bred caddie, Beijing boasts a thriving caddie black market, providing well-forged papers with each caddie sold.

2. Loyalty. This quality is directly proportionate to your caddie's level of dishonesty regarding the rules and your opponent. An important factor in this regard is the depth of your caddie's wallet. Let it be said that lack of ethics is preferred.

3. Skill. Not only must your caddie carry the clubs—he must carry them *well*. He must carry them with pride, ability, and precision. He must *bear* them as Atlas bore the weight of the world.

---

[23]Such as that ball drop which is more of a ball *pitch*, as it rolls a good thirty yards *toward* the hole.

TRADITIONAL CART NOISE ABATEMENT SYSTEM...

3

Battle Dress: Matching Your Spiked Sandals with Your Sweater Vest

The golf course (and its accompanying Pro Shop) is the only place in society where a man can wear a lime green kimono with pink spiked sandals and not be shunned as a social outcast for it. Attire holds great spiritual significance for the True Golfer. The theory of the Ancients holds that different colors will affect the body's energies in different ways, and that, to quote Li Po, "Of all the colors of the spectrum, it is they that are brightest and most offensive that will extract the most power for things Golf." Or as the great Tu Fu once told me, "If I'm not wearing magenta plaid, I'm not playing!"

The other advantage, of course, is that the brighter colors and more thematically complex patterns have been proven to cause debilitating—even permanent—retinal damage. This is best exemplified by the ancient myth of Ping Po[24], he of the Vengeful Plus Fours. Look it up, it's a great story.[25]

The type of attire worn while playing golf is not only specified in the Rules of Golf but can also prove an effective part of your defensive and (obviously) your offensive strategy:

1. Paisley, plaid, striped, dotted, or otherwise visually impairing and noxious garb. As I have said before, never underestimate the power of clothing to offend, disable, and otherwise cripple your opponent. Note that your opponent may also have this tactic in mind. I suggest you bring a seeing-eye dog with you on the links, just in case.

2. Spiked sandals or slippers. Much has been said about these already, so I will only add that ten-inch heels with fishnet stockings look stunning.

3. Plus Fours, or Knickers. This more recent garment has become terribly fab of late. They are silly-looking trousers that end just below the knee and make the wearer look rather like a molting, pregnant ostrich. They will go the way of the Pet Rock Chipped from the Great Wall.

---

[24]This myth has, of course, been adapted by Christianity into the story of St. Orville Moody, Patron Saint of Golfers, who taught the lepers of the lower Colonic Valley in Peru how to golf without hands.

[25]See Appendix for our translation of "Ping Po's Lucky Day."

⦿ OFFENSIVE BATTLE DRESS...

4. "Year of the" Shirts. These comfy cotton jerkins are sweat absorbent and suitable for formal occasions (such as state dinners and executions) as well as sport. They feature the animal being celebrated for the current year in a little design over the left breast. Smashing![26]

5. The Sweater Vest. Whose idea was this anyway? What do these things do?

Anyway. . . .

---

[26]The "Year of the" shirts have survived through the centuries and evolved into the alligator, turtle, frog, polo player (Year of the Polo Player?), etc., shirts that nauseate so many Westerners today.

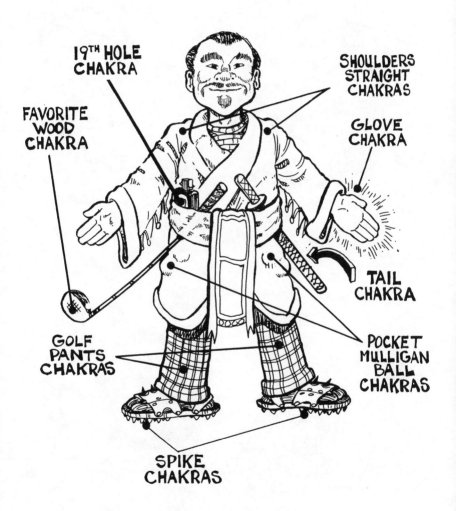

GOLF CHAKRAS.

RESPECTING THE FIELD OF BATTLE BY
REPLACING ALL DIVOTS–.

4

The Field of Battle:
The Teeing Ground, the Fairway,
the Rough, the Holy Green,
the Hole, and the Pro Shop

The ground of a golf course can be divided into seven categories: the teeing ground, the rough, the fairway, the hazards, the Holy Green, the hole, and the Pro Shop. It is very important to master these thoroughly, for you are not only engaged in life-threatening combat with your opponent, but you are also battling the very ground upon which you walk. The ground is your enemy, but you must treat it with respect. Throughout all your travels remember that the best tactic is that which will leave the ground intact. To ruin it is inferior. This is called "replacing your divots."

The Teeing Ground: This is the one true no-man's-land of golf. You and your opponent come to the

box naked and unproven, with no strokes handed out to either player. The only advantage tendered at this point is The Honor, meaning who is to be the first to drive. It is wise to let your opponent drive first so that you may observe his technique and skill. Unfortunately, your opponent may also have read this paragraph, and thus the honor of who is to drive first is determined by a contest of panda wrestling—he who pins his panda to the mat first drives second.

The Fairway: What is to be said? It's the fairway.

The Rough: This is where you should ambush and kill your opponent if you have any intention of doing so. If, however, you intend to play the hole out to its humiliating conclusion and leave your opponent alive to beat you on yet another day, then this is where you will spend many fruitless hours searching for your lost ball while thinking to yourself such thoughts as "Is this poison ivy? It looks like poison ivy" or "I could be killing my opponent now."

The Hazards. The Nine Varieties of Hazard shall be discussed in the following chapter.[27] Skip them at your own risk.

---

[27]The continuous fracturing of short chapters into still shorter chapters was standard policy for all writers working for Harper-Woo Publishers, Inc. They were, it should be noted, paid as much for white space as they were for words.

The Green. The Holy Green can be said to be the castle walls over which every Golf Warrior must climb. It is the sporting world's metaphor for the temple of vestal virgins, with the hole inviting, the grass lush and fertile, and the erect pole showing the way. The pole is topped with a flag that flutters in a cooling breeze, a banner calling to all those with a full set of Wu Li Snead Clubs. It is the Buddhistic Plane of All That Is Golf. Most never reach it (at least not under par), but they continue to try, and it is in the trying, of course, that the meaning of Golf is found.

The Hole. Were I so capable or literate I could wax poetic and metaphoric about the hole and its many resonating images.[28] It is the gateway to the afterlife, the symbol of fertility, the path we must take to inner knowledge. But this is all old hat, isn't it? Enough said, right? Oh, and if you tend to overputt, have your partner stand on the other side of the hole to block for you. A zone defense is more effective than man-to-man.

The Pro Shop. The Buddhist will say that all life is suffering, the Taoist will say that life's hardships are but lessons on the road to higher life, the Confucians will say, "If the Master said it, it must be true." Verily, all of these men have experienced the Pro Shop.

---

[28]See Sigmund Freud's *A Psycho-Sexual Study on Golf*, in which he elaborates upon what he calls "The Pole-in-the-Hole Syndrome."

5

The Nine Varieties of Hazard (Animate, Inanimate, and Dead)

The hazard is that part of the course that is not your enemy yet is designed to harass, anger, and vex you to the point where you will break your Wu Li Snead Clubs (all ninety-three of them) over your knee, thus forcing you to buy yet another set at the Pro Shop. You must approach hazards when you are in a state of peace, or else they will daunt you and plague your stroke. The only problem is that a golfer's mind is *never* at peace; thus it is better to simply go through the hazards like a stampeding herd of llamae.

The Grass. The grass is your very first obstacle. If it is not tended properly, it will snag your ball, entangle your club, and hide decaying mounds of yak patties. As the Master once said, "It is important to hit *over* the grass!"

The Sand Pit. I have little advice to give on this matter. I can only tell you that if you get lost in a sand pit, conserve your water, for the third day out will be the hardest. Do not be reluctant to eat your caddie.[29]

The Water Hazard. Less of a true hazard than a nuisance. It is best to take a philosophical attitude toward the water hazard and mobilize your navy to make an effective strike on your enemy's position.[30]

If this fails, simply drop a new ball over your back—not any closer to the hole than the ball's previous known position.

The Rock Garden. The rock garden is commonly a place of rest and contemplation where a man can be alone with his soul. However, all of these men alone with their souls in an attitude of rest and contemplation while you are trying to play through can be as disturbing as the roar of a butterfly in the next meadow. Kill them.[31]

The Mountain Peak. Go around it, not over it.

---

[29]Just remember to rake the sand pit out before you leave, preferably using concentric circles to form a pattern not unpleasant to the eye.

[30]It seems that Sun Tzu might have written this book at the same time he wrote *The Art of War* and therefore scrambled some of the concepts—but not, we are sure, their meaning.

[31]We recommend you use your pitching wedge.

Packs of Wandering Zen Masters. These tend to congregate on the sunny side of the mountain in springtime, just after the rains. They are not so much a physical hazard, but they will engage the golfer in oxymoronic tests of wisdom sure to enlighten your soul and throw off your swing.

Dead Golfers or Soon-to-Be-Dead Golfers. These are due not only to the precipitous hazards which mark our finest courses but to the impatience of players who are loath to wait for that brand of creature who thinks that golf means stitching a fine pattern back and forth across the fairway in fifteen strokes or more.[32] It is not only possible but probable that the course may be littered—nay, *strewn*—with the bodies of ex-golfers.

Indigenous Fauna. These include unique species such as the angry bald pandas, llamae, meandering yaks (producers of the aforementioned patties), tigers, pelicans, and sumo wrestlers[33].

Occasional Water. Volumes have been written on the many types of occasional water that may be encountered on the course and the proper strategies for

---

[32]We think he means slow, bad golfers who refuse to allow you to play through.

[33]They took a boat.

NEGOTIATING THE CASUAL HAZARD...

dealing with each.[34] Occasional water is easily the most metaphysical of the many hazards you shall encounter, as its vicissitudes and changing moods are random and unplanned, yea, almost *coquettish* in their utter transcendence. Occasional water may drop from the heavens above or be left by wandering oxen or golfers with poor bladders. The Sea of China may on some occasions qualify as occasional water. When it does, all occasional water rules and the various nuances for getting around them shall apply.

---

[34]We recommend *Vardon on Occasional Water*, Rousseau's *Reveries of Lowland Wetness*, B. F. Skinner's *The Interpretation of Puddles*, and Immanuel Kant's *Discourse on Dampness*. At least one great musical work (Handel's *Occasional Water Music*) has also been inspired by this stunning subject.

ENCOUNTERING THE LLAMA HAZARD.

6

Maneuvering: Getting to Here from There

The direct path is not always the best path. As important as hitting the ball, finding the ball, and hitting the ball again is the actual task of walking to the ball. The golf course at Fon Shi, for example, takes well over five weeks to play through, and how you handle the vicissitudes of actually covering that distance can mean the difference between a blister and a hole in the head.

One way in which you might use this space to your advantage is to try to confuse your opponent. If, for example, you bring along a band of fifty bagpipers to see you off in search of your ball, then you will certainly undermine his inner game. Or take the example of the famed Yellow Golfer, who would never just walk off to find his ball but would leave the teeing box doing a nice lively step dance,

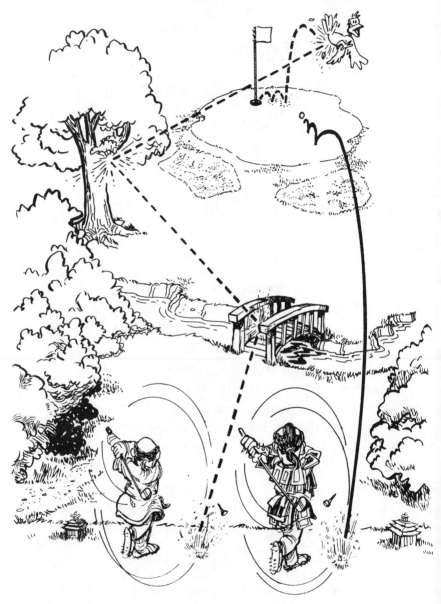

kicking his legs high, throwing back his head, and letting go a jolly laugh.

Truly, he was a great golfer.

But distance is what we were talking about, and as easy as it is to hit your ball five thousand *yi*,[35] it is quite another thing to eat thirty oranges in half an hour. If you slice your ball into the rough, do not feel as though it is a setback. Most likely it is an indirect route that you can put to your advantage. Should you find your ball lying so far from the fairway that its distance may be measured in nautical miles, merely gather your provisions, consult your compass, and set out across the countryside.[36]

When determining your course it is good to consult the omens. These come in many forms. For example, the sound your club makes as it hits the ball can be a telling divination tool.

There are three . . . hold on a second . . . *four* varieties of sound produced when the clubface connects with the ball:

---

[35]The *yi* is an Ancient Chinese unit of distance equal to the length of an oxen's umbilical cord—prebirth.

[36]Just this very thing happened to Mr. McDonald while playing the ninth at the Mao Tse-tung Mini-Golf-O-Rama. He drove off the box out into the Shanghai Bay, hired a boat to retrieve the ball, played through the city's sewer system, and ended up holing out at the eighteenth in one under par. Of course, he skipped holes ten through seventeen, but as these moments of triumph come so seldom to him, we decided to concede McDonald the game. The fact that he was heavily armed at the time had nothing to do with this decision.

1. The driver solidly connects with the ball, sending it winging its way toward a sure par: this is called the Bellowing Of The Bull Moose.[37]

2. The driver hits the ball slightly off center yet connects nonetheless: this is called the Sigh Of The Homoerotic Mule.[38]

3. The driver merely skins the side of the ball, sending it into a spiraling slice not unlike the downward motion of a flushed toilet: this is called the Circumcision Cry Of The Newborn Monkey.[39]

4. The driver connects with a well-sized pocket of air molecules: this is called the Escaping Flatulence Of The Wild Hare.[40]

This is invaluable advice, but I will waive my consulting fee. Remember non sequitur.

---

[37]Translation of this passage was particularly difficult, as Sun Tzu frequently used onomatopoeia. For example, the "Bull Moose" reference might be more accurately rendered as "thunk."

[38]"Schhlooorrppp"

[39]"Rrrpppssshhhllckckckckck."

[40]Actually, *this* is the sound of one hand clapping in the dark.

7

Void and Actuality:
Hitting the Ball
and Not Hitting the Ball

Many have been the words written on golf, but few have been those written on hitting the ball and its converse—not hitting the ball.

Hitting the ball is sublime ecstasy. Whether driving 250 yards or chipping fifty feet to the green, hitting the ball is an affirmation of reality. Therefore it is called "actuality."

Not hitting the ball—often called "slicing air," "hooking the atmosphere," or just "whiffing"—is the absence of these traits. When a golfer fails to keep his left arm straight or does not keep his eye on the ball, his energy is spent on nothing. He connects with nothing. He realizes nothing. *He is nothing!* This state, therefore, is called "void."

There is not enough that can be said about hitting the ball in the game of golf. Hitting the ball, after all, is what drives the game. It is what you *do*.

ANATOMY OF A WHIFF.

It is what the game is *about*. Therefore, if you hit the ball, and hit it well, you will have few problems in golf. This is called "obvious."

Not hitting the ball, however, will prove more problematic. These, therefore, are the four things that you must do if you do not hit the ball but still wish to win the hole.

1. After whiffing for the first time say, "Okay, now I am ready to take my shot." This will get by most opponents at least once.

2. Tell your opponent that the ball on the tee is an illusion, as is all life, and that the actual shot is placed nicely on a little rise twenty *yi*[41] short of the green (be sure to dispatch your caddie to make it so). Tell your opponent that a Zen Master told you, "The ball that is hit does not always gloat; the ball that is not hit does not always take it well."

3. Refer to the height of your club in disparaging tones, such as, "This club is too short!"

4. Chastise your enemy for distracting you during your swing. If he claims he was silent, say "Your *breathing* was disrupting the delicate balance of silences and the movement of air." Order him to hold his breath during your swing. This has manifold ramifications, as by the third hole your oppo-

---

[41]The *yi* is an Ancient Chinese unit of measurement roughly equivalent to the distance a snail can crawl in an eighth of a fortnight.

nent will likely be suffering from oxygen depletion, thereby decreasing his motor coordination and strategic ability by a substantial-enough amount to theoretically double his handicap.

There are times when one does not hit the ball; and rather than actually swinging through nothing, one scoops out a well-sized divot and sends it flying with the grace of a peahen to where it lands, six inches from the hole. One's ball, on the other hand, will have moved less than a foot, backward. My only advice in this instance is to play that divot out.

Sometimes, with especially bad players and especially soft sod, the ball may enter a state known as The Negative Arc, when, instead of whiffing or divoting, the golfer will drive the ball *into the ground* as though driving a rail spike into the Beijing & Shanghai Line. The player is *not allowed to move the ball*, but instead is required to dig a trench three feet in diameter around said ball. It is for this reason that some golf carts, known as Whiffer Specials, come equipped with backhoes.

Finally, if you are attempting to drive but just cannot seem to meet that annoying requirement of having the clubface actually connect with the ball, you are, after seven consecutive misses, allowed to throw the ball at the green. I recommend you throw a spitter.

ADDRESSING THE BALL.

8

The Posture
of the Golfer

Generally, management of your club is similar to management of a vast army. Thus, to direct the clubface against the ball (perpendicular and with just enough lift) is the same as overrunning an enemy's capital city, selling his army into slavery, burning his weapons, and tearing up his library card.[42] It is all a matter of organization.

Remember, the deluge of water does not move the boulder because of its strength alone but because of the way in which that strength is directed. For example, you might think it would be impossible for the Yellow River to move a twenty-ton rock.

---

[42]The editors (and their lawyers) would like to make the disclaimer that this last is *not* considered appropriate behavior on a modern, civilized golf course. Although in New Jersey . . .

And you would be right—*unless the river used a 9-iron, stood away from the rock, kept its head still, and maintained a swing plane perpendicular to the ground!* In which case the Yellow River could paste that boulder into the next province, probably holing out in one under par. Thus you see the importance of posture to the game of golf.

For the True Golfer there are very few elements that make up what might be called good posture. But these few, when mastered, provide an infinite spectrum of kinetic possibility. Remember, there are only five notes in music, but the obnoxious cacophony that these notes can produce is endless.[43] If I had one *yi*[44] for every piece of musical trash that I hear at the Imperial Ball, then I certainly would not have to spend my time writing books such as this.

Still, I am writing such a book, and I suppose you expect some advice on . . . what was this chapter? . . . oh, yes—posture. Okay, here's what I have to say about posture:

Keep your head still! Don't twist your hips! What are you twisting your hips for? That would be

---

[43]Sun Tzu is obviously clueless as far as music is concerned: there are certainly more than five notes in the musical spectrum. They are the whole note, the half note, the eighth note, the sixteenth note, the thirty-second note, the sixty-forth note, and the one hundred twenty-eighth note. But not, of course, the two hundred fifty-sixth note—only a bonehead would use that one.

[44]The *yi* is an Ancient Chinese monetary unit roughly equal to five bales of hay (Japanese).

fine it this were a dance, but it's golf! Don't twist your hips in golf! You swing the club like you were trying to swat flies! Is that a swing plane or are you pretending to be a helicopter?! And follow through. *Follow through! If I have to tell you again I'll stab you with a wooden stick! Do you want to live in Hackerstown, kid? Is that it? You know where Hackerstown is, don't you, kid?*[45] *It's where all the bad golfers live! If you don't want to go to Hackerstown then follow through!*

Never mind. I give up. You're hopeless. *A total failure!*

For you, the path to becoming a True Golfer will be long and arduous. In fact, it might be well nigh impossible. But there is hope. As you know, there are more ways to win at golf than actually hitting the ball. For some of the best of those ways, consult my next chapter.

As the Master says, "Stay out of Hackerstown, kid."

---

[45] Hackerstown, in 500 B.C., was located on the Baishui River, just north of the Kingdom of Shu. It was actually *part* of the Kingdom of Shu, until the bad golfers started buying up all the real estate. Thus went the neighborhood.

9

Tactics: Offensive (and I Mean *Really* Offensive) Strategies

As I mentioned in my chapter on waging golf, it will often come to be that a golfer has the same chance of winning a round as the nude, shorn panda has of finding a tweed pantsuit that will fit him in the hips. This is the time when the golfer, no matter how pure his karma or how accurate his clubs, will have to resort to subterfuge and deception—perhaps even overt sabotage. This can be done in many ways that do not involve actual murder (though murder is, of course, always an option). Although this is hardly a comprehensive accounting of the *other* methods of the True Golfer, I myself have had great success with the following five Offensive Tactics:

1. The Phlegm Offensive. This requires the Golfer to store up a reserve of juicy, bilious phlegm over the course of several holes, and then loudly cough up said phlegm just as the opponent is at the height of his swing plane. This is called "hacking up phlegm." Without fail, this will cause your opponent to miss the ball while simultaneously wrenching his back and sending him scurrying to the nearest acupuncturist.

2. The Wife Offensive. Just as your opponent is about to swing, mention that you didn't realize his wife had been taking private lessons from the House Pro out behind the potting shed. Say you overheard the following line: "You hold my putter very well, dear, just remember to keep your wrist . . . ahhhhh . . . supple."

3. Compliment Your Opponent's Ensemble. This is done by saying something like "Gee, Chu, you look really gorgeous in that matching robe and slippers. I *love* the way it fits you in the crotch." This will probably end your game by default, as your opponent will do one of two things:

> **a.** attempt to kill you by doing the ancient Dance of the Furious Golfer on your face with his spiked slippers

> **b.** suggest sneaking behind the clubhouse and having you "make a man out of him"

4. Offer to Give Your Opponent Some Pointers After the Game. This is accomplished by saying something like, "Gee, Wu, you've got quite a hitch in your swing. Maybe, I could help you straighten that out." Say this after every swing and you will surely debilitate him as he wonders how long he's had that damn hitch in his swing and how he can get rid of it.

5. The Caddie Offensive. Bring a caddie who has just taken a freshman course in Zen studies (such as Cryptic Dialogues Without Form or Meaning 101). He should be encouraged to make quiet comments to you that your opponent can also hear, such as "Did you see his aura? It's got a hole big enough to chip through!" After one or two such remarks, your opponent should be so concerned about chipping through his aura that he will begin consistently doubling par. The other advantage of this offensive is that your caddie will engage the Wandering Packs of Zen Masters (see Hazards), thus freeing you to putt in the pleasant void of your own soul.

6. Boiling Oil. Remind your caddie to bring along his two-hundred gallon vat of boiling oil.[46] If it looks as though your opponent is going to crush you like the maggot you are, utilize the oil appropriately. Try to keep any oil spillage in the rough so as not to damage the fairway or the green.

---

[46]We found that 10-40 weight works best.

There are other Offensive Strategies that one might use (such as the classic "Waggling Buttocks Offensive"), but the True Golfer must experiment and search to find those methods of duplicity that are most compatible with his own karma.

10

Doctrine:
The Rules of Golf

The rules are the most important aspect of golf, more important than the club, the ball, the players, or the course. The rules are all. Before the rules, there was nothing. Without at least several thousand rules golf would just be a lot of men in funny clothes chasing a little white ball through the grass with sticks.[47]

Using the rules to your advantage often means finding a path through their loopholes while snaring your opponent in their manifold traps. Caution is recommended, as fiddling with the rules creates some very slippery slop. These, then, are the 326 considerations that you should take into account regarding the doctrine of golf as they have been

---

[47]Similar to croquet, but not as fast moving and arduous.

designated by the Most High Guy Who Makes Up These Rules.

1. Teeing. The first rule of golf states that the tee must be placed *on the ground.*

2. Getting the Ball to the Hole. What do you want? A diagram?

3. Club Throwing. Aim to kill. As the rules state, you won't get a second shot.

4. Putting. Neither you nor your caddy may physically alter the course of the ball once it has been struck. You may, however, chase after it, doing the Astral Dance Of The Constipated Golfer. Remember to perform the ritual chant, "In the hole! In the hole! Go, go, go . . . Ohhhh!"

5. Zen. No golfer shall engage in Zen dialogues while on the green. Any golfer caught trying to start a conversation with the line "What is the sound of one hand clapping in the dark?" shall be shot from a cannon into a bowl of tapioca pudding. You think I am kidding? Try me. You are also not to use the words "feeling" or "intuiting."

6. Divination. Use of the I-Ching in game fixing or wagering is strictly forbidden; therefore, don't get caught.

7. Reciting Haiku While Driving. Don't even *think* about it. I *hate* haiku.

8. Ball Droppings. Always curb your ball.

⟐TEEING THE BALL—.

9. Lightning. Should monsoon-type winds bear down on the course and vicious streaks of lightning threaten your very life, *you must play through*! Should lightning strike, merely make sure your opponent or your caddy is the highest object in the area.

10-325. Ball Cleaning. These 316 rules have to do with the myriad ways of cleaning your ball. Look them up. They're a scream.[48]

326. Club. Number 3 wood, definitely.

Oddly enough, that last bit of advice—about the 3-wood—concisely sums up my Total Philosophy regarding golf. It always amazes me how the grandest subjects can be captured in the simplest of phrases. Like this whole Zen thing that's currently

---

[48]Unfortunately, no copies of the legendary volume of ancient Chinese golf rules (*5,137 Scrolls to Golf By—Or Else*) have survived to the present day. In fact, only two references to this fine work have been documented at all. The first appears in the emperor Wi Lei's account of the Great Toilet Paper Shortage. (His insight into the comfort level of faux leather bindings is particularly brilliant.) The second reference is actually a rumor that the scrolls were brought to Europe by Marco Polo, who later set a teleological fire raging through the Vatican when he offhandedly wondered aloud how many golf rules might be inscribed on the head of a pin. When the answer, "two," was definitively arrived at, the pope burned the scrolls and changed the subject of the question to some blather about dancing angels.

STAYING SAFE FROM LIGHTNING_.

sweeping the country. They keep asking, "What's the sound of one hand clapping?" and then snootily looking about as if to say, "Oh, ho, don't have an answer for *that*, do you?" But they never get to the crux of the matter and talk about *why* only one hand is clapping. Is there no other hand? Or is the other hand simply not participating, petulantly withholding service for the sake of some clever monk's ego?

Golf is the same way, I find. Therefore, I will leave you with this final word on the waging of Golf: when you next get quizzed about some particularly obtuse point of Golf-ania, go for the simplest, grandest most unarguable of answers. Say, "Number 3 wood, definitely."

You will have them.

Appendix

Ping Po's Lucky Day

*E*ditors' Note: The following tale was discovered at a dig in Anhui in the tomb of a Han nobleman and dates from the second century B.C. It was inked on silk in the outlawed lishu style of characters and wrapped around the dead nobleman's favorite ball, which was placed inside his chest cavity, close to his heart. Said noble was buried with a full set of Wu Li Snead Clubs (the Autograph Series), which hints at royalty.

Ping Po sat on the mountain and wept. His tears brought forth water hazards, and his cries, sounding like the dulcet tones of Tibetan bells, distracted putters throughout the land. Finally after years of this agony and missed putts, the Great Greenskeeper climbed the mountain and asked Ping Po, "What is the matter?" And he wailed this song:

"I am in love with the unattainable. My chip shots are off, my putts are dropping, and my balls are blue."

"How did you lose her?" asked the Greens-keeper.

"It was a bet. Best two out of three holes at the Tiananmen Mini-Golf Hut. I lost to the Palace Pro."

"That truly is tragic."

Ping Po scowled, "Oh, thanks, that cheered me up! I think I will just lay down on the green, pull the turf over my head like a blanket, and sleep the sleep of the truly fozzled. Keep me well watered and be sure to post a 'no chipping' sign over my body."

"Take heart, Total Failure, and fear not," said the Greenskeeper. "I will get help." And he climbed down the mountain while Ping Po, wallowing in embarrassing amounts of self-pity, continued to wail and annoy the countryside.

So the Great Greenskeeper went to Gertrude, Goddess of Golf, who sat imperially in her throne under the Crest Of The Crossed Clubs, and told her of Ping Po's tale of woe.

"Ha!" she said, holding a tee in one hand, a driver in the other, and a wedgie in the third, "You call that woe? I've seen more woe in Sun Tzu's writings of golf."

"But Gertrude," the Greenskeeper said, "he's threatening to lie down on the green and just gently decompose into the turf. It's rather *off-putting*, don't you think?"

She killed him.

Then the Goddess of Golf made her proclamation.

"Okay, I shall do something, but only because bad golfers make for horrible fertilizer."

When Gertrude came to the weeping and wretched Ping Po she was immediately filled with sympathy and scorn.

She said, "Snap out of it, you pathetic little son of a bastard weasel."

"Are weasels illegitimate?" he asked.

She struck him thrice upon the collarbone.

"Thanks," said Ping Po, "I needed that. But, oh, my Good Goddess, what shall I do? My love is away from me, and I think it is time for me to—"

"Yeah, right, lie down on the turf and rot away. I heard already. That's a great way to win back a woman. Fine strategy there. *Think*, you protozoic little tick."

He asked, "Are ticks protozoic?"

"Think!"

He thought.

It didn't work.

"Look," she said, and he looked but saw nothing.

"Where?"

"It was rhetorical, you bonehead. Just shut up! Are you *totally* lacking in communication skills? Wait."

He waited.

And there before him, hovering in the clouds like a fuzzy kite struck by lightning, a strange shape materialized.

"What the hell is that?" he asked.

"Lo, these are the Most Mighty and Magical"—she paused with a goddesslike flair for the dramatic—"*Vengeful Plus Fours.*"

A hush befell the world. Angels wept. Choirs sang *Plus Fooouuuurs! Plus Fooouuuurs!*

"Wow," Ping Po said, and he meant it. "Great production values."

"Merely don them and ye shall have great power during all encounters on the links, you insignificant scab on the buttocks of lichen."

"Do lichen have buttocks?" he asked.

"Do you want to find out?" she answered.

He withdrew the question.

"Close your eyes," she said.

He did, wondering what it might be like to be a scab on the buttocks of a lichen.

Suddenly, there was a tingling on his thighs and crotch, an almost quivering sensation of power and obnoxicity. He looked down and saw wrapped about his legs the most offensive and garish pair of plus fours ever to disgrace the human form.

"Wow," he said, and he meant it.

"Go forth, you scabrous son of a molting she-goat, and win the hand of your woman—and keep your decomposing flesh off our golf courses."

"Do she-goats molt?" he asked.

Gertrude tried her best to keep from whacking Ping Po upside the skull with her driver—and failed.

"Go!" she shouted, and he goed, wrapping a robe about his waist to hide the glow from his Most

Vengeful Plus Fours.

At the Tiananmen Mini-Golf Hut, by the soda machines, Ping Po found his True Love with his True Rival, Fong Fu.

"Fong Fu, second cousin of your aunt's father, I challenge you," said the powerfully dressed Ping Po.

"You don't challenge me at all," Fu scoffed.

"Eighteen holes. Putters and astroturf!"

Fong Fu stood up. Ping Po stared at him.

Fong Fu said, "Do your worst!"

Ping Po replied, "I will!"

The game was not lengthy. Ping Po, feeling an inappropriate burst of pride, played the first hole straight. Fong Fu holed out in one. Ping Po played six before he made it through the windmill.

"Damn," he said, and he meant it.

At the second hole, with the loop-the-loop, Ping Po stood by the mat, preparing to take his shot.

Then he said, "Gosh, it's hot. Let me take off my robe."

At which time he unwrapped his overgarment and shed the light of Gertrude's Vengeful Plus Fours upon the world.

The burst of colors rivaled the experience one gets when opening a box of Lucky Charms (the old kind, with the yellow marshmallow moons). Dementia struck everyone on the course. Even those on the driving range were scathed by the plaid demons.

Fong Fu merely said, "Some knickers." Then

he imploded like a summer grapefruit under the heel of a Carthaginian elephant.[48]

Ping Po looked to his True Love, also writhing from the experience of the VPF.

"Now you are mine!" he said.

"Keep it in your pants, Ping Po," she said scornfully, before melting like a poorly designed fudgesicle.

Ping Po was nonplussed. He merely procured a watervac and stored his True Love in a vase on the mantle, right next to his framed receipt of his first down payment on a complete set (all ninety-three of them) of Wu Li Snead Clubs.

She was his.

The End

---

[48]See Livy, *The Game with Hannibal* (copyright 60 B.C.).

Sun Tzu's Ancient Art of Golf™
was brought to you by the people at
Wu Li Snead Clubs.
"If you're not playing with Wu Li Sneads, you're
not playing."
This has been a paid endorsement.

Sun Tzu's Ancient Art of Golf™
is a trademark of
McChapin McMerchandising Unlimited,
so don't even *think* about slapping it on
a T-shirt without their permission.

The True End

Golf Addenda

For those who doubt the truth and reliability of our discovery of this great lost work by Sun Tzu, we offer as proof other "lost" golf anecdotes from history. These include those fascinating historical sidelights that are often left out by undiscriminating scholars, nongolfers, and bitter whiffers. Only recently have such stories come to light, and we think they complement this book quite nicely. (Plus, the publisher wanted more pages, and we couldn't think of anything else.)

Biblical Apocrypha About Golf

One of the most astonishing discoveries made upon the release of the Dead Sea Scrolls[1] was this hitherto unknown passage from the second chapter of the Book of Genesis. Some call it *Apocrypha*, which means "of doubtful authenticity," but, frankly, few sections of the Bible are as obviously authentic as these.[2]

---

[1]Or, as we prefer to call them, the Dead Water-Hazard Scrolls.

[2]We understand that God has a vastly huge negative handicap. See Jesus' autobiography, the tell-all potboiler *Driving from the Mount: Memoirs of My Games with Dad.*

14. And on the tenth day God said, Let there be Golf, and there was Golf. 15. And God saw that it was Good, and God said, Let us make The Golfer in Our Own image, after Our Own likeness. 16. And He took some turf, some sand, and a little rough, and He molded it in His hands, and thus created The Golfer. 17. And The Golfer lived in happiness, wanting nothing. 18. And he was without sin until his first double-bogey whereupon God cast The Golfer from Paradise and gave him the name of Hacker, and cursed him, and said that He would crawl across bunkers and fairways, chasing a ball and never coming in under par. 19. And when The Golfer was removed from Paradise, he noticed his nakedness, and was shamed, and went immediately to the Pro Shop to put a whole new wardrobe on his Amex Gold Card. 20. This is the word of God.

Golf Myth and Legend from Around the World

As Immanuel Kant said: "Where Golf is, religion cannot be far behind." And he never said anything truer! In our relentless scouring of obscure sources known to none but us, we came across these deities and heroes wrapped up in the life-and-death battle that is Golf:

Glossmarrl—Germanic God of the Driver, whose clubs were forged in the legendary Pro Shop of the dwarf Ixlex. Glossmarrl figures heavily in the *Saga of the Icelandic Long-Distance Relay Putters*, in which Thorvald Ericcsonn is revealed to have putted eight hundred miles across the Greenland tundra to discover Detroit, only to lose his ball before holing out in Toledo.

Lundestrupa—Celtic Goddess of The Relentless Whiffer, who created the Celtic ritual of keening—those long mournful wails of agony that make the Celts so fun at parties. The first reported incident of keening is said to have occurred when the mighty Cuchulainn, doing what he so often did (that wacky guy), decapitated his golfing partner, Monty, for no reason at all. Does he need a reason? He's Cuchulainn.

Trickster Tales of Golf (Navajo)—Coyote, it is said, drove off the long sixteenth at Paha Sapa with a sand wedge. Such a card, that Coyote. He was also known to occasionally disguise himself as a caddie and recommend putters for extricating balls from bunkers. Oh ho, quite a knee-slapper, there.

Xqllxllacalcoatl—Aztec hero associated with introducing the first ball game into ancient Aztec society. In this game opponents engaged in deadly combat in order to put small balls into even smaller holes[3].

---

[3]At first we wondered why the holes were smaller than the balls, but then we realized that the game was thought up by Quetzalcoatl, and we all know what kind of guy *he* was.

Plutarch's Handicaps

Only the most ignorant of savages[4] do not know who the great Roman historian Plutarch (A.D. 46–120) was. His *Lives* was a rippling bestseller in ancient Rome[5], but his lesser-known works have languished in pitiful obscurity. One such work is *Plutarch's Handicaps*. Here are some choice tidbits:

"Veni, vidi, rimi.[6]"
> —Julius Caesar

"Friends, Pros, countrymen, lend me your clubs.
I come to play golf, not to praise it.
The balls that men slice live on after them.
The long drives they hit are soon forgotten."
> —Marc Antony

"Plato is dear to me, but dearer still is golf."
> —Aristotle

"If I were not Alexander, I would be Mike The Golf pro."
> —Alexander the Great

---

[4]Tennis players, for instance.

[5]Number one with bullet on the *Roman Times* Bestsellers List. Of course, with only one person out of every ten thousand able to read, four copies made a bestseller. *You* try thumbing through a fifty-foot-long scroll on the subway.

[6]Loosely translated: "I came, I saw, I holed out."

"That's a great swing if you're an Emperor, but this is golf. Sure, you can conquer the world, but can you do it under par?"

—Mike The Golf Pro, to Alexander

Golf in Ancient Rome

From Livy's *The History of Rome: The War with Hannibal:*

Most historians think—erroneously, we now know—that Hannibal crossed the Alps during the Second Punic War to attack the Romans. Hannibal (which translates as "don't handle my balls"), that great Carthaginian leader of yore, was actually attempting to play a ball lost when his elephant, suffering an allergic reaction to Hannibal's new aftershave, sneezed his ball into the Alps.[7] He only attacked and slaughtered millions of Romans because they tittered when he bogied over Padua. They never laughed at a golfer again.

---

[7]In ancient Carthage it was common practice to use elephants not only as caddies but also as makeshift tees—the ball was placed on the tip of their trunks. This truly is the only time in history when elephants were not only allowed on the fairway but were socially acceptable alternatives to the golf cart.